Houdini
and
other Masters
of Magic

By
Jan Fortman

A

Book

From
RAINTREE CHILDRENS BOOKS
Milwaukee • Toronto • Melbourne • London

Library of Congress Number: 77-12638

Art and Photo Credits

Cover illustration by Lynn Sweat.
Illustrations on pages 5, 10, 13, 15, 21, 28, 30, 35, 38, and 46, Sam Viviano.
Photos on pages 9 and 41, Wide World Photos, Inc.
Photos on pages 19 and 44, The Granger Collection, New York.
Photos on pages 23, 24, and 32, courtesy of the New York Public Library.
All photo research for this book was provided by Sherry Olan.
Every effort has been made to trace the ownership of all copyrighted material in this book and to obtain permission for its use.

Library of Congress Cataloging in Publication Data

Fortman, Janis L. 1949-
    Houdini and other masters of magic.
    SUMMARY: Highlights the lives and careers of magicians Doug Henning, Robert-Houdin, John Henry Anderson, Alexander Herrmann, and Houdini.
    1. Magicians—Biography—Juvenile literature. 2. Conjuring—Juvenile literature. [1. Magicians] I. Title.
    GV1545.A2F67   793.8'092'2 [B] [920]   77-12638
    ISBN 0-8172-1032-6 lib. bdg.

Manufactured in the United States of America
ISBN 0-1872-1032-6

Contents

Chapter 1

The
Rock Magician
DOUG HENNING

People talk and laugh with one another as they wait for the show to begin. As the lights dim, everyone becomes quiet. A band begins to play rock music. The great stage curtains open, and a smiling Doug Henning walks onto the stage. You can feel excitement in the air as the audience waits to be amazed by Henning's first trick.

The stage lights brighten. There, in the center of the stage, is a young woman. She stands in an open sack, the cloth gathered about her feet. Her hands are locked in handcuffs. Henning lifts the sack all around her and neatly ties the top. He steps aside. Suddenly, the audience gasps. The woman is now standing on the stage, out of the sack, and without handcuffs. Henning is now inside the tied sack, handcuffed! Henning and the woman have switched places without anyone in the audience ever seeing a thing! A trick—an *illusion*, you say! Of course, you must be right! *But how does he do it*? Half the world would like to know, but Doug Henning won't tell.

When the young Canadian magician was six years old, he saw a magic act on television. The magician made a woman float in the air! Young Henning was amazed. How could a woman float in the air? A few years later, he got a magic set for his birthday. He learned how to do many magic tricks from books. He read all the magic books he could find. Soon he was doing tricks for everyone.

When he was 14 years old, Doug Henning did some magic tricks at a birthday party. He was paid five dollars. After that, he put an ad in the newspaper. It read: "Have Rabbit, Will Travel." Henning gave magic shows at birthday parties, in coffeehouses, and at rock festivals.

Henning later worked his way through college by giving magic shows. After college, he received a grant from the Canadian government to study magic. He traveled all over the world to study with master magicians.

One night Henning gave a performance at a rock concert. A great idea was born. He would put together a new kind of magic show—one that combined magic and rock music! Two producers came to see Henning's show, called *Spellbound*. They loved it and brought it to New York. They gave the show a new name— *The Magic Show*. During the show Henning performs many great illusions to the beat of rock music. He makes people appear and disappear at will, and he makes objects float around the stage. He even turns a dove into a rabbit.

In one act, a woman wearing black tights comes onto the stage. She smiles at the audience and then lies down in a painted wooden box. Henning closes the box. Only the woman's head and feet stick out. Henning grabs his saw and wildly cuts the box in half. The woman screams out in pain. The audience is uneasy. Some cover their eyes, others wipe damp faces, *all* jump a bit from their seats.

When the box is completely sawed in two, Henning moves the two halves apart. Several people in the audience scream. One woman faints, and her husband fans her. The head of Henning's assistant is sticking out of one half of the box. Her toes are sticking out of the other half. *Is she alive?* Yes, her toes are wriggling! Every shirt in the audience is soaking wet, every mouth cotton-dry. When Henning finally brings his "victim" together again, the audience applauds wildly.

But Doug Henning is only "warming up" for the *big* illusion! A large, steel cage is wheeled onto the stage. A smiling woman appears and steps carefully inside the cage, as Henning locks the door behind her. Then he covers the cage with a large silk cloth. It's easy to figure out what happens next—or is it? If you think the woman disappears, you're right. A few moments later Henning takes away the cloth. The woman is

Henning looks pleased after "sawing a woman in half."

In the woman's place in the cage is a snarling cougar.

gone! But now, inside the cage, a large, growling cougar is pacing back and forth!

How does Henning do it? No one knows for sure, and it seems certain Doug Henning will never tell. As a matter of fact, he made everyone in *The Magic Show* swear they would never tell the secrets of his tricks. All Henning will say is that the hand is *not* quicker than the eye. He makes people believe that what they are *seeing* is really happening. He believes the magic, says Henning, so the audience believes it.

Imagine yourself watching an elephant carry a man across the stage. Suddenly, right before your eyes, the elephant disappears. The man on its back falls to the floor with a crash.

Chances are, the man on the floor is Doug Henning. He has just made you *think* he was sitting on a huge animal's back. The animal vanished, and Henning no longer had anything on which to sit. Doug Henning creates *magical illusions*—what you see is *not* what is really happening.

If the year were 1920, the performer might have been another master of magic called *The Great Houdini*. If, instead, we were living in the middle of the 1800s, the magician might have been a French master called Robert-Houdin, from whom Houdini later took his name.

In the last 200 years or so, thousands of magicians have amazed people all over the world with their tricks, *sleight of hand* (the hand is quicker than the eye!), and illusions. We have chosen five of these magicians as the best. Their stories are told in this book. You have just read about one of them—Doug Henning, "The Rock Magician." In the following chapters are the stories of "The Greatest Magician Who Ever Lived," "The Great Escape Artist," "The Wizard of the North," and "Herrmann the Great."

Ladies and gentlemen—this theater takes great pride in presenting, for your amazement and delight, the super . . . the incredible . . . the absolutely unbelievable . . .
MASTERS OF MAGIC!!!

Chapter 2

The Greatest Magician Who Ever Lived
ROBERT-HOUDIN

Jean Robert spent much of his young life in Blois, France, training to become a watchmaker. It was his father's craft and now it would be his. Then one day, there came an accident in his life that would change his whole future.

While Jean had worked and studied long hours to become a watchmaker, he had a hobby that he loved even more than his work. *Jean was a magician.* He read every magic book he could find. Card tricks were his favorites, but he did many other tricks as well. One night, to help a magician friend who was ill, Jean agreed to appear in a magic show in his friend's place. *Life would never be the same again for Jean Robert.*

The theater was packed when Jean walked on stage and began doing the card tricks he knew so well. The crowd loved the tricks and clapped wildly. Then Jean tried some of the tricks he'd watched other magicians do. The first few tricks went so well that Jean became bolder —and a bit foolish for a beginner. He tried his friend's famous *Omelet Trick*. He asked a man in the audience for his hat. While Jean was talking, he secretly placed a cooked omelet inside the hat.

Before the eyes of the audience, Jean mixed some eggs, milk, salt, and pepper together and poured the mixture into the hat. What the audience didn't know was that he had already placed a hidden container inside the hat.

Next, Jean simply held the hat over a flame, pretending to cook the egg mixture. As he did this, Jean talked to the audience at the same time. But Jean was so nervous, he didn't watch what he was doing. The hat burst into flames! The audience burst into laughter. Everyone laughed at the young magician's mistake—ev-

Suddenly Jean found he had cooked not only the eggs but the hat as well.

eryone except the man whose hat had just gone up in smoke!

Jean had learned an important lesson from that first show. It takes years of practice to become a great magician. Though he was still interested in magic, Jean decided it was safer to go back to Blois and make watches for a while.

In Blois he continued to spend all his free time practicing his magic tricks. He also met and married Josephe Cecile Houdin. Jean added his wife's name to his and became Robert-Houdin.

At the age of 40, Robert-Houdin's 20-year-old dream came true. He again became a magician. His opening show was in July of that year, 17 years after his first disaster in show business. Luckily, this show went better. He had figured out exactly *when* to make the secret moves. The years of practice had paid off. *Robert-Houdin was becoming a master magician.*

Robert-Houdin liked electrical and mechanical tricks. In the 1800s people knew little about electricity. It hadn't yet been put to use for anything, and so his tricks were especially mystifying. He would use electro-magnets (the electro-magnet had only just been invented), trap doors—anything that would surprise and excite the audience. Robert-Houdin became famous throughout Europe. His shows were filled with a kind of magic no one had seen before.

But Robert-Houdin's last performance as a magician may have been his greatest magic act. *He was asked by the French government to prevent a war!*

From 1844 to 1860 France had control over Morocco—a country in northwest Africa. People called *marabouts* were impressing the superstitious Moroccans with feats of magic. The marabouts were a religious people who claimed they had supernatural powers. Their "magic" was probably done through clever illusions, but the Moroccans thought the marabouts were supernatural beings. The marabouts were advising the Moroccans to revolt against the French. The French government asked Robert-Houdin to perform magic tricks for the Moroccans that were even greater and more mysterious than those of the marabouts.

Robert-Houdin had a hard time coming up with the right magical trick to meet the difficult challenge. He went over the most difficult acts he had ever done. None seemed good enough.

Then, he came up with an idea. He laughed as he thought of it. Here was the simplest trick he knew, and yet it just might work. No, it *would* work. He would show the Moroccans his *Light and Heavy Chest* trick and they would be amazed!

As Robert-Houdin entered the tent, he was more than nervous. His hands trembled. All around the tent sat the audience—the most important leaders in Morocco. He felt them sneering at this European magician who claimed to have more powerful magic than the holy men (the marabouts).

Robert-Houdin placed a small box on the stage. He turned to the Moroccans and said, "At my will this box becomes light or heavy. I challenge the strongest of you to come and lift the box." A burly Moroccan man came onto the stage. He lifted the box easily, laughed, and showed his friends how he could hold the box high over his head.

Robert-Houdin smiled and said to the man, "I will now take your strength away. The box will become heavy, and you will not be able to lift it."

With all his might the strong Moroccan tried to lift the chest.

The man just laughed and said, "You cannot take my strength away!" He put the box down and was about to walk off the stage. The audience started for the door. Robert-Houdin shouted his challenge again. "This box will be too heavy for even the most powerful man in Morocco!" This time, the man couldn't move it off the floor. He tried again and again. His face reddened, his muscles strained as he pulled at the chest. The results were the same. The man just couldn't lift the chest.

There was a good reason that the Moroccan couldn't lift the chest. Hercules himself could not have moved it. Before the show, Robert-Houdin had placed an electro-magnet beneath the box. When an assistant turned on the switch, the magnet held the box to the floor. When the switch was turned off, the box became "light" once again.

Robert-Houdin performed many other fantastic tricks in Morocco. He made a man disappear, and he caught a bullet in an apple. All in all, he convinced the Moroccans that French magicians were better than the marabouts. The revolt against France soon ended. After that, Robert-Houdin called himself "The Greatest Magician Who Ever Lived." Maybe he was also the greatest French diplomat of all time.

Chapter 3

The Wizard of the North
JOHN HENRY ANDERSON

John Henry Anderson was born on a farm near Aberdeen, Scotland, in 1814. By the age of 17, John Henry was a pretty fair juggler. Watching hundreds of performers over the years, he had learned juggling and some magic tricks as well. He had learned while watching from the best place of all—*behind the theater curtain.*

Since he was 10 years old, John Henry had a job with a traveling theater company. His parents had both died, and John Henry moved from town to town helping to set up the stage and the theater, running errands for the actors, assisting the cook—anything that would keep him near the magicians who were part of the show.

After seven years of road shows, John Henry decided he was ready to strike out on his own. He had saved enough money to hire a small town hall and several actors for a play. As a special feature, he would do a few magic tricks. He was, after all, quite young. How could he do a whole magic act by himself and expect people to pay to see it?

Anderson needn't have worried. He was not just good, he was *great*! The audience loved his tricks, and he soon was putting on a whole show of magic. He brought his magic to dinner parties

Anderson performed for delighted audiences throughout Europe.

and theaters throughout England and the rest of
Europe. Everywhere, people were talking about
the wonder of John Henry Anderson, master of
magic.

For someone who had grown up the hard
way, there came an evening in his life when

John Henry felt he was the luckiest young man alive. One of the people who came to see him perform was Sir Walter Scott, the author. Because he had written so many books, Sir Walter Scott was known to all as the "Wizard of the North." At the end of the show the famous

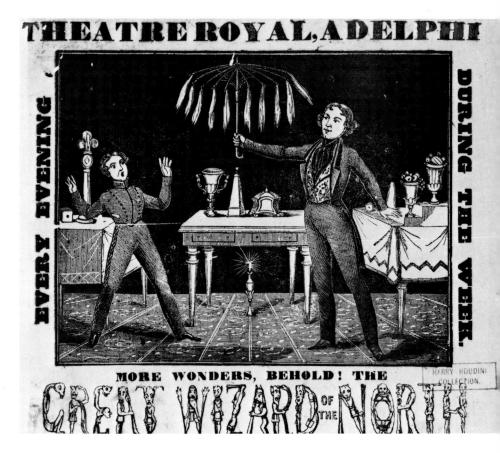

An original poster advertising "The Wizard of the North."

writer came backstage. "Good evening," Sir Walter said, smiling broadly. "Mr. Anderson, your magic is wonderful. I have never seen a greater magician! To me, sir, *you* are the Wizard of the North from now on."

In 1840 Anderson appeared at the Theatre Royal Adelphi in London. People had waited in long lines for hours to see "The Wizard of the North" perform his world-famous tricks. They were not disappointed.

First, Anderson did his *Magic Caldron Trick*. On the stage was a large pot held up by chains over a fire. The great magician showed the audience that the pot was empty. Then he poured water into it and dropped some dead pigeons into the water.

The water boiled. Anderson stirred the boiling brew and said, "I will make the pigeons come to life!" The magician stepped back, said a few magic words, and the pigeons flew from the pot! The birds flew out over the audience and back to the stage. The audience exploded in applause and cheers. How did he do it? Was it really magic? But "The Wizard of the North" was just getting started. He had planned a new trick as the feature of his act. The "Wizard" was now going to be shot by a gun and *catch the bullet in his bare hands*!

Anderson asked someone in the audience to come up to the stage. A bullet was marked and shown to the audience and to the man who had joined the magician on the stage. The man checked the bullet and assured the audience the bullet was a real one. Then the bullet was loaded into the gun. Anderson gave the gun to the man, walked to the other side of the stage, and politely told the man, "Now, sir, please aim the gun at my heart and pull the trigger."

If anyone in the audience breathed at that moment, no one heard the sound. The man on stage was trembling so, he could hardly hold the gun. Anderson had to calm him before the act could go on. Finally, the gun fired with a roar that rushed through the theater.

Everyone looked at the magician, but Anderson didn't fall over. He just stood staring straight ahead, holding his hands over his heart. The man with the gun couldn't bear the suspense. What had he just done? He anxiously walked over to the magician who still stood in place, staring. Very slowly, Anderson took his hands away from his heart. Holding one hand out, he showed the man the bullet.

"Is this the same bullet that was loaded into the gun? Is this the bullet you fired?" Anderson asked the man.

"Yes, yes," said the man, relieved to hear the magician's voice again. The man examined the bullet. "It has the exact same marks." For several seconds, there was no sound from the audience. Everyone had been so frightened at first, and so puzzled at this point, they forgot to applaud. Then, suddenly, loud cheers went up throughout the theater. "The Wizard of the North" had again done the impossible. *He had caught a speeding bullet in his bare hands!*

Did Anderson really catch the bullet that was fired at him? No, that would have been impossible. Then how did he do it? Anderson had made a special clay bullet that was exactly the same size as the real bullet. He had shown the man the real bullet, but when Anderson loaded the gun, he actually put in the clay bullet. He hid the real bullet in his palm.

When the man fired the gun, the clay bullet simply exploded inside the gun. It made a great

Had Anderson really caught a speeding bullet
in his bare hands?

noise, but no bullet ever left the gun. Anderson
simply pretended to catch the bullet. The bullet
he showed the man *was* the real bullet. It had
been hidden in the magician's palm all the time.

"The Wizard of the North" was a fine magician, but most of Anderson's tricks were not original. They had been done before by other magicians. What was different about Anderson was his *style*. He was an actor, and he was able to make his shows *seem* spectacular.

In the late 1800s sleight-of-hand tricks were giving way to a new kind of stage magic—the *illusion*. A new performer—the illusionist—was now trying to convince people that what they *thought* they were seeing, they were *really* seeing.

Chapter 4

The Master of Illusion
ALEXANDER HERRMANN

Alexander Herrmann was raised on magic! His older brother, Carl, was a famous magician who entertained kings and queens around the world. When Carl's assistant became ill just before his show was to tour Russia, he asked his younger brother, Alexander, if he would help in the magic act. What do you think was the answer of the little boy who dreamed of someday becoming "The Great Alexander"?

For the next three years, from the time he was 12 until he became 15, Alexander thought his dream might be coming true. As his brother's assistant, he toured everywhere with the magic show. He learned Carl's tricks so well, he was becoming an accomplished magician himself. He became so good that he finally traveled to Spain to do a magic show for the queen. She had invited him after Alexander had written her a letter claiming to know a magician as good as his brother, Carl Herrmann. Of course, that magician turned out to be himself!

Alexander was soon performing his magic in countries throughout Europe. Often the two Herrmann brothers would work together, but it was becoming clear that Alexander was no longer just as good as his brother Carl.

Alexander Herrmann was becoming a master of illusion.

Alexander was much better! Not only was he doing the sleight-of-hand tricks Carl had taught him, but he was making up new ones, too. He was also becoming interested in the magic of illusion—making people believe that what they *think* they see is really happening.

In 1874, after being held over in a London theater for almost three years, Alexander

Herrmann left for a tour of the United States. He met a pretty ballet dancer while sailing across the Atlantic. Within three months after they arrived in New York, Alexander and Adelaide Scarsez, the dancer, were married. Adelaide became his assistant in the act.

Herrmann's act was a great success in America. One after another, he performed amazing tricks. He turned coins into candy, pulled rabbits out of empty hats, and made things disappear. He wore a special coat with over 20 pounds of trick hardware hidden in it. It wasn't long before Alexander Herrmann was the most famous magician in America. People were calling him "Herrmann the Great." But it wasn't simply his sleight of hand that made him so popular. Alexander and Adelaide had invented a new and special illusion that came at the end of their act. It was terrific!

You are seated in a darkened theater in Chicago. A voice calls out from the stage: *"Ladies and gentlemen. Here is the act you've all been waiting for. Herrmann the Great will make a beautiful woman appear out of thin air! He will cut off her head—and then restore it! Then, she will disappear! Ladies and gentlemen, Herrmann the Great!"*

There is applause, and then the theater becomes stone quiet. The curtains open. The back wall of the stage is covered by a black velvet curtain. The stage is empty except for Herrmann the Great. He is dressed in white—white gloves, white suit, and even a white top hat. The stage is dark, except for a single light on the magician.

Herrmann snaps his fingers and suddenly Adelaide appears out of nowhere! She, too, wears white. A chair appears, and Adelaide sits down. Herrmann suddenly draws a knife from the air and in one clean swipe cuts off his wife's head! You jump in your seat. It can't be, but she is— Adelaide, without a head! She is still alive, thank heaven! Her long white dress is moving. But look at "Hermann the Great." He is holding poor Adelaide's head in his hands.

Now the great magician walks slowly across the stage, still carrying his wife's head. He is talking to it—he really is talking to it! And Adelaide's head is answering him! Do you believe your ears? Do you believe your eyes? Her body is sitting in the center of the stage, while her head is talking on the other side of the stage!

Herrmann picks up the head and slowly walks back to Adelaide's body. He puts the head

As difficult as it is to believe, there is Herrmann carrying Adelaide's head across the stage.

back on her shoulders. She certainly looks better with her head on. But, wait! Where has Adelaide gone? She has vanished right before your eyes. And there goes her chair—gone into thin air! The stage is empty again, except for the great magician. What an act! Herrmann bows and the audience goes wild. They love Herrmann the Great—master of illusion.

Of course, what you have just *seen* hasn't really happened. The illusion was done with black velvet screens and hoods that matched the black velvet curtains in the back of the stage. Adelaide and the chair were on the stage right from the beginning, hidden by black velvet screens. Because there were no lights on the back of the stage, the black screens blended in with the back curtain and couldn't be seen.

When Adelaide and the chair seemed to appear out of nowhere, Herrmann had simply had the black screens removed. This was done without the audience noticing that any screens were even there!

What about Adelaide's head? Actually, a large black screen extended all the way from where Adelaide was sitting to the other side of the stage. The screen was a few feet high.

Adelaide was not really wearing a white dress. The white dress hung on wires in front of the black screen. Adelaide sat inside the dress. It was open in the back so she could slip out.

Herrmann pretended to slice off her head. Then he started to carry it across the stage. At that point, Adelaide simply moved out from behind the white dress and walked behind the black screen. Only her head could be seen because it was above the screen. Herrmann put his hands under her chin, and it looked as if he were carrying her head. An assistant dressed in black moved the white dress to make it appear that Adelaide's body was in it. Audiences everywhere loved this exciting trick.

While Herrmann the Great was amazing America with his magic, a young American boy was just starting life in Appleton, Wisconsin. It was 1874. The boy's name was Ehrich—Ehrich Weiss. You may have heard about him after he became known to the world by another name —Houdini.

Houdini thrilled the world with a new brand of magic—*the great escape.*

Chapter 5

The Great Escape Artist
HARRY HOUDINI

When Ehrich Weiss was 17 years old, he read a book about Robert-Houdin. Ehrich decided he wanted to be a magician just like Robert-Houdin. He decided to call himself "Houdini"—Harry Houdini.

In 1899 Houdini was a struggling young magician. He performed in small-town shows, but he wasn't very successful. Either he wasn't good, or people were tired of magicians pulling rabbits from hats. He decided to try doing an escape act. He had himself tied in tightly knotted ropes. Then, in seconds, in full view of the audience, he freed himself.

A New York theater producer named Martin Beck saw Houdini's escape act in St. Paul, Minnesota. After the show, Beck came up to Houdini. "You have a nice act, son, but escaping from a bunch of knots isn't going to make you famous. Can you get out of anything else?" Beck asked Houdini. "Can you get out of a pair of locked handcuffs?

"Sure," Houdini answered. "I can get out of anything."

Beck thought Houdini was just bragging. He promised to come by after the next day's show.

He did, and brought with him a pair of hand-cuffs. "I borrowed these from the police," Beck said as he snapped the handcuffs on Houdini's wrists. "I'll put the key in my pocket. If you can get out of these handcuffs, you've got a job."

Houdini turned his back to Beck. It took him less than one minute to open the handcuffs. Smiling, Houdini turned to Beck and handed him the handcuffs. On the spot Beck decided to feature Houdini in a traveling magic act— "Houdini, The Great Escape Artist."

Houdini's tour took him to every part of America. Everywhere, he challenged his audiences to bring a lock he couldn't open, a trap from which he couldn't free himself. In each city he appeared he challenged the police to provide handcuffs or a jail that would hold him. But no one could keep Houdini prisoner. The world was learning that *The Great Escape Artist* seemed, indeed, to be able to get out of anything.

But Houdini knew people would become tired of the handcuff act. He had to think of more exciting kinds of escapes. One of the earliest he dreamed up was the *Milk Can Escape*. The first time he tried it on the stage, the the-

Houdini in chains, handcuffs, and leg shackles.

41

ater was packed. In the center of the stage was a milk can large enough for a man to squeeze inside. Houdini walked out on the stage in a bathing suit. He called several people up from the audience.

"Please check this milk can," Houdini told the people on the stage. "Make sure nothing is hidden inside. Make sure the locks my assistant will use really do lock, and that there is no way to unlock them from *inside* the can."

As the people returned to their seats, the milk can was filled to the brim with water. Houdini jumped from a ladder into the can with a splash. Water spilled out over the sides of the can. Then he brought his head down and his assistant placed the top on the can and locked it to the sides of the can with large, heavy locks. Finally, the milk can was covered with a cabinet.

Silently, the audience waited. No one stirred. Every eye watched for some movement. Every ear listened for a sound. But nothing seemed to be happening. The only sound was the ticking of a clock. A minute passed, then two —and still no sound, no movement. Three minutes passed. The suspense was maddening!

Suddenly, Houdini burst from the cabinet. Soaking wet, he bowed to the cheering audience. He brought up his hand, pointing to the milk can. *Incredibly, the can was still locked*!

How had Houdini escaped? How could he have opened the can without opening the locks? The answer is simple. Houdini never bothered to open the locks. The milk can was built in a special way. There was only one way to open it —from the inside. Once inside, Houdini pushed against the top of the can. The upper section of the can was made to lift, locks and all, from the lower part of the can. Lifting the top required all of his strength plus the pressure of the water around him. As Houdini rose out of the water, the level of the water fell in the can, so little water splashed from the can as the top section came off.

But Houdini's greatest act was probably his escape from the *Chinese Water Torture Cabinet*.

In the center of the stage was a large, tall cabinet. The front of the cabinet was glass, covering strong steel bars that made the cabinet an "escape-proof" prison. The whole cabinet was filled with water.

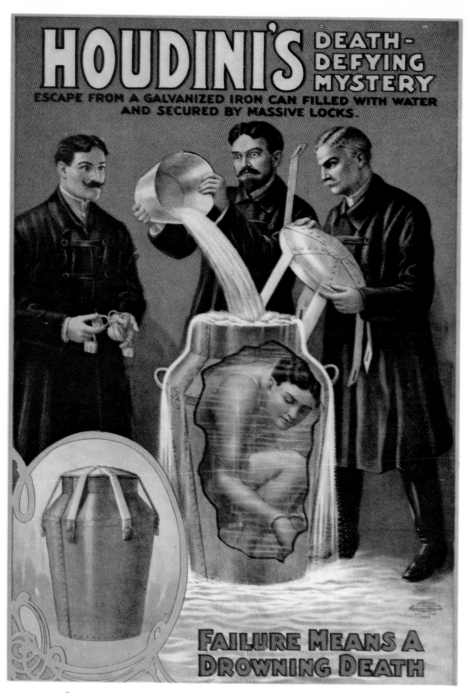

Original poster for performance of Houdini's milk can trick.

As in the *Milk Can* act, Houdini stepped out on stage in a bathing suit. But this time his ankles were locked in a pair of chains. Houdini's assistant hooked the leg irons on the famous escape artist to a hoist and raised him, upside-down, over the cabinet. Then Houdini was placed, *still upside-down*, in the water cabinet. The chains on Houdini's feet were locked to the top of the cabinet, then the top was set in place and locked on. The audience could see Houdini, hanging upside-down in the locked, water-filled cabinet. Then the assistant placed a curtain around it.

The orchestra began to play as everyone waited in suspense. Houdini's assistant stood next to the cell and peered inside occasionally. In case anything went wrong, he had an ax waiting. He would smash the glass with the ax and let the water pour out. But the ax was never needed. Nothing ever went wrong with this trick on stage.

As always, Houdini built the suspense and made the audience wait. A minute passed, then two, then three. The orchestra kept playing, and the audience kept their eyes on the curtain, waiting. All of a sudden, the curtain was opened. Houdini appeared, dripping wet and smiling.

After thunderous applause, he asked a group of people from the audience to come up to check the cabinet. They reported to the audience—it was still locked!

How did Houdini, chained upside-down, escape from the water-filled cabinet?

Here's one idea on how Houdini escaped from his watery prison: Once inside the cabinet, Houdini bent upward. Holding onto the bars, he pulled himself up with his hands until his head was above the surface of the water.

Remember—as in the *Milk Can* escape, when Houdini's body was lowered into the tank, much water splashed out of the tank. This left an air space between the surface of the water and the cover of the tank. Lifting his head into the air space, Houdini could breathe.

Houdini then unlocked the lock with one of his many master keys (Houdini had an unbelievable set of master keys that fit just about any lock or pair of handcuffs made) and freed his feet. He released an inside lock that held the top section of the cabinet to the bottom and climbed out. Then he replaced the top of the cabinet and came out to greet the cheering audience.

Through the years, Houdini kept the secret of this trick closely guarded. For years after Houdini's death, other magicians tried to imitate this trick, but they didn't know exactly how Houdini did it. Houdini was then, and is remembered to this day, as "The Great Escape

Artist" and one of the world's foremost masters of magic.

Between Houdin and Henning, the world has praised many performers as "masters of magic." We chose just five for this book. You may be thinking of some magician you have seen who does even more wonderful tricks than these. That may be. There will *always* be new magicians to replace the old. Perhaps there is even one future master of magic reading a book about the old masters right now!

920
For

Fortman, Jan 80-256

Houdini and other
masters of magic

NOV 17	DATE DUE		
APR 1			
JUN 14			
APR 21			
OCT 19			
JAN 13	Darland		
JAN 13			
Mar.13			
MAR 19			